WHO AM I?

I am swift and silent, fierce and feathered.
I hunt at night.

WHO AM I?

By Moira Butterfield
Illustrated by Wayne Ford

Belitha Press

First published in the UK in 1996 by
Belitha Press Limited, London House,
Great Eastern Wharf, Parkgate Road,
London SW11 4NQ

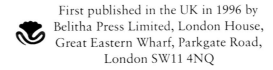

ISBN 1 85561 576 2 (hardback)
ISBN 1 85561 705 6 (paperback)

British Library in Cataloguing in Publication Data for this book
is available from the British Library.

Printed in Hong Kong

Editor: Jilly MacLeod
Designer: Helen James
Illustrator: Wayne Ford / Wildlife Art Agency
Consultant: Andrew Branson

I have feathers and a beak
And long sharp talons on my feet.
I hunt at night with shining eyes.
People say I'm very wise.

Who am I?

Here is my eye

My eyes are big and round. They help me see in the dark. I like to hunt at night and sleep during the day.

I sit quietly in the shadows watching for small, tasty animals to run by. I will catch them and eat them if I can.

Here is my head

My ears are hidden
under my feathers.
I can hear very well.
I listen for squeaking
and rustling noises.

I can hear something
moving in the grass
below. It had better
watch out. Can
you see what
it is?

Here is my wing

My wings are very long. When I see something to eat, I spread my wings and fly very quietly through the night.

The mouse does not hear me coming. When I am overhead, I swoop down and grab it. Then I carry it back to my home.

Here are my talons

My talons are long
sharp claws on the
end of my toes.
I use them to catch
food. I can grip very
tightly with them.

When I sit in a tree,
I curl my talons
tightly around a
branch. I can sleep
for hours sitting
up like this.

Here are my feathers

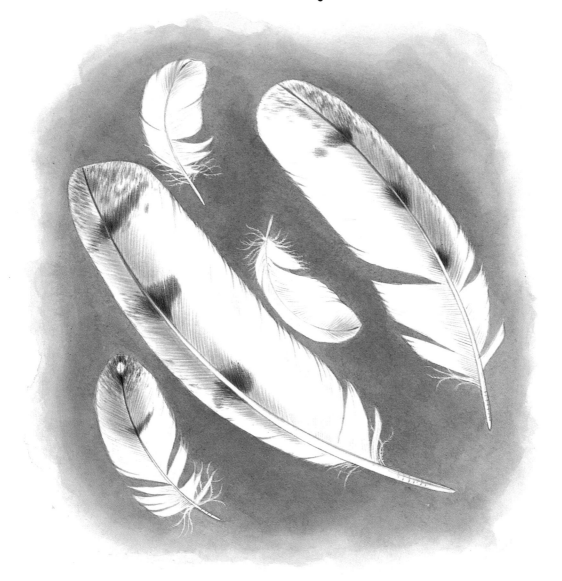

I have long speckled feathers on my back and wings. The feathers on my tummy are short, white and fluffy.

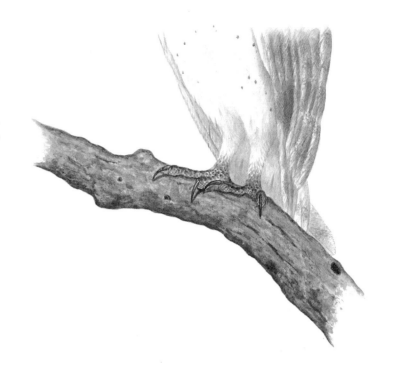

Sometimes I clean my feathers by splashing in a puddle. Then I find a safe place to sit and dry out.

Here is my beak

I use it to tear my food into little pieces small enough for me to swallow. I only like to eat meat.

I often eat fur or bones but I don't like them. So I cough them up again, squeezed together in little balls called pellets.

Here is my home

It may be inside a hole in a tree
or in a quiet building. Sometimes
I warn other birds to stay
away from my home.

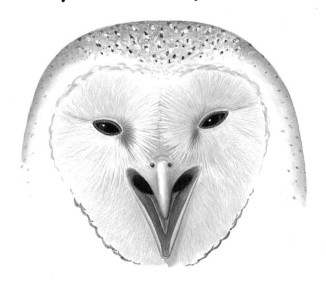

I open my beak and…
screech!
Have you guessed who I am?

I am an owl

Point to my ...

sharp talons

round eyes

pointed beak

long wings

white tummy

speckled feathers

I am called
a barn owl.

Here are my babies

They are called
chicks or owlets.
At first they cannot
fly. I go hunting
and bring them
food to eat.

Slowly my owlets
grow until they are
big enough to fly
away. Next year
I will have some
more babies.

Here is my territory

It's the
place
where I live
and hunt for food.

Can you see a mouse, a bat, two frogs, three rabbits, and a beetle?

Here is a map of the world

I live in lots of different countries. Can you see some of the places where I live?

Can you point to the place where you live?

North America

South America

The places where
I live are this colour.

Europe

Africa

India

Australia

Can you answer these questions about me?

Do I hunt during the day or in the night?

Can I see in the dark?

What do I like to eat?

What are my claws called?

Do my feathers all look the same?

Do I have any ears?

Where do I make
my home?

What are my babies
called?

Do I sleep lying down?

Here are some words to learn about me

feather Feathers are made up of lots of tiny soft fluffy strands. I have some long ones and some short ones.

glide When I stretch my wings wide and float softly along.

owlet A name for a baby owl.

pellet A little rounded ball made up of fur and bones from my last meal. I cough up pellets every day.

plunge When I swoop down very fast.

screech The rather strange noise I make. Can you make a screeching noise like me?

speckled Coloured with lots of tiny dots, like my wing feathers.

talons My long sharp claws. I have four on each foot.

territory The place where I live. I often live in grasslands and hunt for food on the edge of woods.